Annus Mirabilis

Winner of the Barrow Street Press Poetry Prize
selected by Ellen Bryant Voigt

Annus Mirabilis

SALLY BALL

Barrow Street Press
New York City

Designed by Robert Drummond

Cover photo:
©2004, Carol Panaro-Smith /James Hajicek
Earth Vegetation/04-1
Photogenic Drawing on Vellum
Alchemy-Studio.net

Author photo: T. M. McNally

Published by Barrow Street Press
Distributed by:
      Barrow Street
      P.O. Box 1831
      Murray Hill Station
      New York, NY 10156

First Edition

Library of Congress Control Number: 2005908922

ISBN 0-9728302-4-3

For my family, near and far–

Contents

There are many causes and varieties of beauty;
he that can prove them is so much the more to be trusted.

−Albrecht Dürer

Mealy Redpole

Drawn from Nature and on Stone:
he perches on a finger of a branch,
shaded in from nowhere;
enough sky appears around him
to indicate the air, the palest wash
of blue. Watercolor.
Linaria canescens–he's like a sparrow
with a scarlet brow. It took two artists to render him,
J. & E. Gould: naturalists forgiving
his cocking and winking and articulate
craning as he held his pose.
They focused on markings, fold of wing, reptilian angles
of his tiny claws, the line dividing
upper and lower beak–a line that unless
perfectly made would force an attitude:
sad bird, angry bird, bird gravely disappointed....

From the Goulds' recording Hullmandel
could make his print. To him was left the universe
in which to represent a Mealy Redpole: he chose
the length of bough, the strange patch
of sky. He wanted, of course, to highlight
what they'd made; also, though, to draw
the viewer in, to make a space
so tantalizing it wasn't scientific.
Not for the bird. He didn't love the bird.

1652

Like all the Saxon children, Leibniz sorts through leaves.
Today he's with his mother, stiffly dressed. They sit
beneath a sycamore and he selects

eligible leaves for her to hold together
in a small bouquet. Yellow, green, and brown,
a single red one, a few of the yellows stippled

with green like drops of ink seeped
into a handkerchief. He's six and his father
died this year. His mother can't manage all the leaves,

and lets some go, which Leibniz doesn't notice.
Then, absentmindedly, she takes
a desiccated one he's offering and lets it go,

and he is furious. Yes, yes, she says,
and takes it up, and a few minutes later
makes the same mistake.

These desiccated leaves are small clenched hands,
but the ones she likes, the ones anyone would choose,
are rubbery and strong and as big as Leibniz's head.

She fans his face with their collection, a little tickle,
a bit of tenderness. He smiles and looking toward her
reaches for the ground; he checks his purchase

on the leaf he'd seen, and holds it by himself. Curiosity
and certainty collide: he knows he was making something
patterned, something whole–not what it was–and now it's gone.

Proofs

Heartbeat + Caffeine = Hyperbole
Or: Heart + Caffeine = Access to Restricted Areas.

In the news today, Clara Barton's untouched
Missing Soldiers Office found preserved, full of inexplicable bolts
of black fabric. Then they discover a photograph:

the black swagged out the windows
for Lincoln's funeral procession.

Also: octopi can be taught
to open jars of food. If the lid
is too tight, they strain, turn red,
eyes bulging, using four tentacles.

Heart + News + Caffeine = What do these things weigh

together, what do they weigh?

The soldiers' mothers' searching . . .

Clara making lists, accounting for the numbers of the dead,

the historians mystified by the voluminous
cloth, solving for X:

the procession, the funeral of the commander–

All that faith and effort, like the octopus

so satisfied and smart with his open jar . . .

The solution is always a nourishment in itself.

Given

I have no facility for this, am just
intoxicated–Fermat's "very great number
of exceedingly beautiful
theorems."   Conviction
as trajectory, vertigo +
finitude:

       running downhill, or
catching sight of stars,
                  sudden constellation
in a sky wild with racing clouds.

I want another lens, or
I want to see the lens itself,
the one Newton made,
              his fingers
coated in white dust.

Excursus

Miracles are not to be multiplied beyond necessity.
                              –Gottfried Wilhelm Leibniz

As for philosophy, he colludes in the signification of words,
calling those things miracles which create no wonder.
                              –Isaac Newton

The hands at work in concert with the eye.

As paints are ground from matter,
so are lenses.

How the mind opens and closes,
how it replies to wonder:
sometimes, bedazzled, unconvinced;
others, bedazzled and refreshed.

They both *believed*
in miracles. Which is to wish for them,
to love what cuts away
the known.

Notebook

I. Water and Salt

In this kiln, we add salt to the water
in the form of pellets, to make it gentle.
The humming plastic tub in the garage seeps
its melted lozenges into the house, protecting
the equipment from calcification, our bodies
from soap, from the dust-sodden air.

Water is eaten by light. The cracked sea floor
litters its horde of bones and scales
in the wind. The ocean has turned
to dust and passes over us.

II. Time and Eternity

Time evaporates in the desert. The air
is pavement the color of a robin's egg.
Elsewhere I'd grown used to my moods
mirrored in the heavens, places where the sky
invites ripples or explosions of human urgency.

Not here, not this glare.
When a cactus dies,
it doubles over and disintegrates so fast—
the flesh, then the spindly ribs.
Skinny bent dowels cracking in the sun.

No part of me
is merciless like this. Right?

III. The Old Neighborhood

The sun had gone from the neighbors' brick wall,
which was all I could see of their house, massive, supported
by ancient rusted stars that anchored cords,
with painted bits of trim under the eaves,
and all the thousand-colored bricks, a sea, a moving tide,
going flat and hushed at dusk.

Did I say windowless?

Like the sea

Grown Son

The man opens the flue and crumples
newspapers, stuffing them down
between the dry logs, rolling sections tight
to serve as kindling, positioning each log
then resettling it, just so. He is meticulous.
His father taught him a specific method.

Once it's going, all the air moves toward the fire,
up the chimney. He's thinking of his father,
or his father's legacies: an illness, possibly,
sudden and ruinous, a love of tools and proper ways
to handle projects, daily plans of action.
The man fears for his own mind—he monitors

his physical response to moods, anger or defeat.
He sleeps with his fists clenched, sweating,
concentrating. He loved his father and lost him
at thirteen. So young that now in retrospect
he only guesses how alike they might have been.
For years to love his father's been another story:

he's a shadow, a serene and carefree silhouette
of his old self. He remembers everything,
but happily. It's not forgiveness, it's disease.
One log collapses and the man strikes it,
knocks it into little coals, bits of orange char.
People have felt forgiven who were not. Years of conflict

that can never be resolved, that have stood still
already twenty years. Here, at the very center of his house,
everything flies into the sky. Ashes float
with smoke and air away. He's made this thing,
which burns and hisses, which he feeds.
The whole house empties to the night.

$$f(N) = 6(s + 7)$$

The candle in the glass appears and disappears.

The Candlemas in the glassjaw appears and disappears.

The candlewood in the glasswork appears and disappears.

The caner in the glazier appears and disappears.

The Canis Minor in the glee club appears and disappears.

The cannabis in the glen plaid appears and disappears.

The cannonball in the glim appears and disappears.

_____

Cut that out: in math,
formula generates thought,
oh my idol.

              Here only
stifled soul, for want of spiritual oxygen,

burning, singing,
high-flying in the tiny interstices of a particular plaid.

A small one, tight.

The bomb, unlike a wick, will not flicker back.

Trinket

Japanese ashtray featuring a pink anemone—
perfect release. Three cigarette nooks
serve as fingerholds, and I swing the dish
around and back like a pitcher for the Braves.
I am eight feet from the basement's
cement wall, and suddenly
I see into the future:
chips of china scattered on the floor,
empty hand, and that wave of tallness
coming over me—huge ridiculous person
kneeling to pick up each piece,
trying not to cut her fingers,
maybe mad enough to squeeze one handful
and draw blood. Why
is it every time I almost let things go
I'm jarred forward to the moment I can judge
myself? Stuck clenching
the mean-hearted harmless tray
and whispering aloud,
Mercy, mercy. Always already I'm standing
in the stillness sure to follow.

Violent Motion

Today I'm driving in the rain
on a black slick rural route
that traces a range of scrubby slopes–
an instance of the isolation
I've become addicted to & thwarted from–

absence of voices
absence of tyrannies

Away–I am driving and singing
and drinking water cold as
what is falling from the sky outside.

Inside my body: mountain air
laden with pine and rain.
All the little knots and flux
undone.

Could I be ill?
Never enough of love,
and yet the thrill or bald relief
leaving it behind.

Circus

The raucous blue and yellow tent for weeks
was just a jolt of color in the valley,
a cartoon balloon disrupting the brown and gray
that is our xeriscape (the desert's always brown,
except up very close; every house is brown,
and every building–the streets go brownish gray with dust,
the mountains are brown shoulders cinched in tension
over all of us). But since I was inside
of course the tent has changed:
from inky 2-D interruption
to a taut and pulsing skin
concealing those many bodies–
for I know they're in there,
practicing–

Those twin men or boys,
their bodies so alike and so perfected–
who swung in utter synchronicity
on lines the length of city blocks,
so fast, so wide, so vertiginous for us,
their arcs a kind of thrill and swoon
even as we sat shunted into our chairs
like plants in flats.

And then the twelve or fifteen men
arrayed in orange, red and yellow–
their skins by Odilon Redon. They swung and launched
each other in the sky, one man somersaulting
to statuesque conclusion on the shoulders of another,
while the second human spirit/sprite/pure-motion-and-release
passed over him midair, sailed into a kind of drape,
slid down to take a place among the spotters.
The ingenious dependence: no stars,
or every body was a star, the flying and catching and
flinging and watching–choreography

so fluid and astute.

I don't know what we loved and envied more,
the soaring   ·   or the trust:
flush with skill, with knowledge,
how free they were to soar inside–
and yet beyond–their form. Every man in flames
and free to burn.

Heart Swims Away and Is Lost

Low moon the size of a dinner plate
sitting on the horizon to take your breath away
and dispose of you in a romantic seizure:
turns out it measures the same size
as the nickel at the top of the sky–

we see it so grand and huge because it's out of context,
touching the saguaro-tipped mountain,
or the gutters and electric lines at City Hospital, or trailing
its wet gold trembling reflection across an eastern ocean,
like a tongue headed deep inside you (you in particular).

> Oh, moon: I have just the one
> partner, whose love is a floor
> on which to walk out my life.
> You know how he, too, looks at you.
> How dare you knock me down
> and then not take me?

Creation of the World

You know it from the way your own heart moves
when the heavens open: that first morning, too, it was raining
as the souls collected themselves–

they wanted things they didn't know a word for,
to be deciduous, or matronly, or ectoskeletal.

They had their reasons,
coming as they did out of the sameness
and freedom of the air: constant promise of renewal,
desire to deliver, dislike of fur. They flew into a frenzy
as the better lives were taken.

All of them were eager for a body
and for a wide variety of names: crown vetch,
axseed, *coronilla varia*. Such pretty pink and white!

Imagine how it looked
coming alive, swelling with intention,
the joyous and the bitter souls
suddenly constrained–

weighing anything at all's so different from the spirit form,
so limited: all roots, all lungs. . . .
Ivy climbing walls, gulls trapped inside the ozone,
even cheetahs running hard are finally spent.
What they found was what they'd given up.
Now: the flesh, the rain, the nature of regret.

In Hannover: Clairvoyance

I went in February, in the minor steady rain,
with a sick child. Leibniz's name was everywhere:
his haus, an apothek, the cookie factory.

But only one portrait, no bust or display of his inventions,
his manuscripts or voluminous correspondence.
The house is an office, unavailable.

Much of the city is as he knew it. I followed the stone streets,
crossed the river, went into the market church. My son slumped
in the stroller, too sick to mind. He held a cracker in his hand.

Leibniz traveled often in diplomatic service: Hungary, Illyria,
London, Vienna, Berlin and Paris: coaxing and interpreting,
massing essays and letters and problems for further study.

His rival, Isaac Newton, never saw the sea. In the evening,
my son falls asleep on the bench in the pink and purple pizza house.
The shouts and lights resound around his body.

Tidbits, iotas, molecules of soul. Tomorrow at Herrenhausen
I want to see the fountains—designed by Leibniz,
still operational, reliable—though can they fire their arcs

and droplets in this cold? At the hotel, my son and I
share a lumpy bed: boy tossing and poking,
mother pressed against the wall, looking at it, into it,

as if a person might appear there. Yes.
Mines, fountains, coins: they both made coins.
Leibniz robust in the Harz Mountains, getting into everything;

and Newton as master of the English mint, fixing, fixing—
Their portrait faces stamped and stamped
against my eyes: at the edge of sleep,

fluent in their pragmatic impulses, *it can, I shall,*
it can, I shall, diagnose and solve, a kind of currency
that I can spend, tossing the English coin,

then the Germanic one, into the raised reflecting pool.
On either side of me a man–Leibniz's tufts of hair
mounded high and rippling down below his shoulders;

Newton straining backward, away. *Away.*
Mr. Conviviality and Mr. Singleness of Purpose, fused
by a method of calculation, an obsession with utility,

utility as a radical, elegant gift–
You must leave behind the regulated dream.
Why have I come, if not for that?

Note

*And this perturbation, added to the [one] arising from the inequality
and inclination of the lines, makes the whole perturbation greater.*
                                                        —Isaac Newton

The moon is attracted to the earth.
And to the sun. The sun perturbs
the moon's orbit, pulling the moon
as it pulls the tides,
i.e., always releasing.

Like a tease, though the moon
has no emotions. Button your yellow shirt
to the top. Keep your shoes on.
Love is—yes—elliptical;
because of you I love another more.

Odours and Vapours

I can't stop smelling my children–
my nose in their necks, their hair.
In this way, they are again inside me.

Their bodies are discrete:
one that goes by itself, swims
(his face flat as a moon on the surface of the water)
and bounds and offers affection by his own choice;
and one that is tiny, soft, busy on her blanket
with a purple hippopotamus.

I don't mean to halt them
or contain them–rather I'm eager
for the breaking of my heart.
They are willful. They smell of will.

My son asks, When I grow up to be a man
I'll drive the car? And I say yes,
and he says, Where will you sit?

He is the most solid physical thing on earth.
He walks out of the courtyard like a ghost,
a little mass, a moving press of borders
and edges the sun sets itself against,
and he evaporates, materializes, here, not here,
mine, not mine, governed (as I no longer am?)
by curiosity, desire, faith, and prowess.

Of course I am. But how does one evanescence
hold tightly to another?

Newton's Death Mask

The portraits impose distance:
even 300 years ago, he was more
an emblem than a man.

I prefer the aged 3-D face,
which seems so delicate.
Brow a little furrowed,
almost a smile. He does not
look remotely insecure.
The photo of the death mask
makes me want to touch him
(cheekbone, eyelid)
to close my eyes and press my face
against his face–not the flesh,
but the cool surface of the cast.

Two skulls, touching.
A version of union,
a visitation,
chord from a voice, the lather
of excitement
not mine,
all mine.

Annus Mirabilis

I.

In retrospect there is no side to choose:
in math, Newton was earliest to make the formulas contort and yield
but never told a soul; and Leibniz, a little later,
did the same startling calculations somewhat differently,
and published them, as was his way:
wishing always to improve the world.

What they had in common:
dead fathers
bookishness
rigorous, enormous curiosity
sitting for hours at a stretch in one chair, thinking
not sleeping enough
never marrying
egotism
alchemy
the abandonment of alchemy
bureaucratic service, which made science and philosophy a hobby
coinage
dying out-to-pasture, genius-wise

Isaac, though, was born three months after his father died;
he did not have Leibniz's jolly family years,
no father teaching him to read history *both sacred & profane.*
Isaac arrived *small enough to fit in a quart pot.*
Everyone expected him to die.
His mother moved away when he was three:
remarried, gone until she was a widow
for the second time. A seven-year indoctrination
into solitude. At age nineteen, he made a tabulation of his sins
including, *threatening my father and mother Smith*
to burne them and the house over them.

Curiosity an oblivion to be embraced,
an opportunity for fearlessness, for vanishing.

Why publish? That makes a self instead of losing one.

II.

Insight must be joined to fervour.

III.

Fantasy is helped by good air, fasting, and moderate wine.

IV.

Curiosity a place to live, a battlement,
a universe. And they were not ashamed of it.

V.

Electric pace and heady certainty and otherworldliness—
a definition of pleasure:

Leibniz, who's always earnest, usually full of pomp,
it's hard to imagine him entranced. So well anchored to the world
that he could always get the fervent insight down and pass it on.

Then Newton, hungry, refreshed, a little tipsy:

what kind of fantasy? the undulant many-colored circles that roamed
before his eyes after staring at the sun.

So matter-of-fact, so self-contained.

VI.

There were two years, actually: anni:
Newton had fled the plague away from Cambridge,
to the farm at Woolsthorpe, *in the prime
of my age for invention*. Calculus, optics,
machinery . . . on his own land,
the heir, the patriarch:
i.e., whole days to spend alone.

What is a self but an experiment–
one among many . . . but what it finds
may rise above the viscera

axiom

statue

sonata

the made propels, eradicates the maker.

Leibniz under House Arrest

Oh how I love that he should be a George,
my valet, who knows perfectly well

where we have been, where we find ourselves now.

George, King of the wood market.
George, King of the rued philosophers.

The trouble with intelligence
comes when curiosity has withered.

I shall not wither much more.

I have been so many places. I have tried to solve
real problems in the world—not identify, not bemoan.
It is hard to love
and be loved
when you are thinking all the time.

I shall try
to be alive like this. Alive here.
With George, with a good library.

Memory

If memory be done by characters in the brain yet the soul
remembers too, for She must remember those characters.
                                        –Isaac Newton

Messala Corvinus forgot his own name.
One, by a blow with a stone, forgot all his learning.
Another, by a fall from a horse,
forgot his mother's name and kinfolk.
A young student of Montpellier, by a wound,
lost his memory, so that he was fain to be taught
the letters of the alphabet again.
The like befell a Franciscan friar after a fever.

Messala, the soul–
she knows the faces of your friends,
Barrow's face, and your mother's.
The difficulty lies in believing her.
She does not bother with evidence.

She bears in her pockets notation
and also all the human qualities.

We do not experiment with her:

She must be trusted, followed,
a path in a dark wood, where the trees
are inscribed with faces, with letters,
the imperfect curve of C,
the depth of O
an R like new foliage, the V of a forked elm.

Trusted and pursued.

Toward the Opticks

*I took a bodkin, and put it between my eye and the bone as near to
the backside of my eye as I could: and pressing my eye with the end
of it (so as to make the curvature in my eye) there appeared several
white, dark and coloured circles.*

—Isaac Newton

I'd have dreamed a bodkin
was a paramour.

But Isaac, no.
He wakes me, saying:

After I'd stared too long at the sun—
I needed an implement.
When the knife was still,
if I was also, the circles faded.
But a movement of my eye against the metal
brought the circles back.

One reason I understand what I see
when I see stars derives from here,
from the blade, my eye, yes,
yes my experiment.

Is it the measure of *wanting* to see,
is that your question?

Function of X

I.

X and Y are abroad;
X is going crazy and he wants to kill himself.

He wants to walk under a bus;
he says this matter-of-factly, dull in his eyes.
Y finds the dullness excruciating.
She is alone enough without her native tongue
and then this man, X, a sort of taunt:
the epitome of useless, her protector.

They are artists, though they do not thrive on bad behavior.

The bus seems more alive than X, untrustworthy.

II.

How can one wish to be well?
Such a wish depends
on admitting you are not.
Mania means hopelessness alternating with victory,
the soul perpetually in search of company (how lucky to find it,
what raw gratitude floods the heart and mind when locked
together with another human,
someone equal, someone better
than oneself–).

III.

Visionary clarity descends, an unexpected gift:
the mind alive with worthiness.
Y always thinks that once a problem is identified

it's solved, but *Seize the day* is an injunction for the well, the weak,
the bored. X isn't bored–this is the crux.
He's full of thought and work and conviction
yet he's paralyzed. Weakness? Sickness?
Where's the line? (That line intersects
forgiveness, that line affects evaluation–)

IV.

X has done nothing yet that's in the public record.
Though maybe he has broken Y's heart?
When can you determine
how a wound will heal? X is high and low
and he wants to disappear. In Europe,
can't you disappear?

V.

Why does a man choose fidelity,
or not choose it? What notation
could represent despair
within that formula? What does such a formula
tell us about any one man, X?

Y wants to save him; Y wants to punish him.
X was X once, and now X is one letter
in a long sequence, his lifetime of limits and derivations,
the way addition is just the first application
you learn on the long way into the calculus.
Calculus is better, but addition was so clean–
in primary school textbooks it starts

as union. 1 U 1 = 2
How is it anyone forgets that,
taking marriage for consolation.
X and Y did not forget. They were careful to be two.
Maybe it's the craving to be one, to be that imaginary number–

wouldn't that obliterate the one
drowning in his own mind? If Y is resolutely
Y, who will X spend himself on, who can make him vanish,
who can be 1/X?

They got one over on X, the Swabish merchants.
But maybe it saved him from the bus.
Under a woman is not under a bus.

VI.

The world is full of false and dangerous symbols. Which is why mania
is so attractive to a genius. The acuity, authority.
Take me close to death,
to the hard glare of oblivion, in whose wasting light
a febrile clarity comes. Don't we all know it
sometimes? Keenness of mind, touched by risk or by effacement?
It's the premise of boot camp, the Marines.

VII.

"I started out so well," said X,
implying the problem of the present moment.

VIII.

Y ought to change, too, but how to see a change
as other than plain compromise, subtraction? What change
keeps X from being alone in his repentance—
isn't that the key?
The only lack of faith he's shown
is in Y's ability to also fail.

Could she now?
Fail to forgive?
Fail X
or fail herself?

Are those failures tandem
or either/or?

If Y, then X . . .
If X, then Y . . .

This is what you forfeit when you love
everything around a weak spot:
your own must be eradicated or dismissed.

Good-bye. You can always get down to zero,
to obliteration. The only way to strive
is toward infinity.

I want you well.
I want you smart.
I want you back.

Some choices are made utterly alone.

Gravity and Levity

What does anything weigh?
Heide fell in a building under construction—
a temporary staircase collapsed, casting her
against a steel buttress. She said her wrist broke
as if someone had taken an axe to it,
longitudinally.

She writes, "Look who can't stop trying to be special,"
which untucks a laugh I had suppressed:

Heide in flight, loose in the air in her perfect suit. . . .

Funny because of the wish to shield?

She didn't even tell me when it happened,
but six months later, when an amaryllis
I'd given her last Christmas bloomed suddenly,
having seemed to be dead, after her fifth surgery,
"a little note from you."

I can't imagine who attended her, how they lifted her,
if she wept or even cried out. Except the whoop
when the platform gave way:

a sound she'd make in willingness
to excoriate poor workmanship,
or willingness to have a little fun,
a ski slope whoop.

Then shame; irritation.
I want to go and take her to dinner: wine and lamb
in that second-story restaurant she likes—
her raucous laughter, and the cast
at rest there on the tablecloth,
her other hand a leaf, a phrase in the air.

Ascent

1. Modern Medicine

My father needs new lungs, and he is big,
he's tall, so luckily he will get them quickly,
or quicker than most:

many lungs are too big for many lung-needers;
my father should fly right up The List.
Rather, someone's lungs will likely fly right down.

2. Ingenuity

He has:
> hooked up his oxygen to the rack of his 1961 Lambretta motor
> scooter (saved from his postgraduate tour of Europe with his
> brother, Uncle Ed, pre-Vietnam, premarital, pre-everything that
> makes him who he wants to be today: i.e. the plumbing supply
> house, the family, the modest but comfortable life). The tank is
> bungee-corded to the back; my son sits on the front, the forward
> seat, bicycle-helmeted, ecstatic, his hands on the inside of the
> handlebars, his curved back arching a little to touch my
> father's chest. I used to arch my back, also, sitting there.

3. The List

You get to choose, when they call you,
you get to choose whether tonight
you want to get new lungs.

Surely for people sick in bed it's worse.
Or maybe not: they're surely going to die, and soon, so it's not a choice.
They just say yes and get the transplant.

Though of course, he's on the list.
just being *on the list.* . . .

I sometimes think about his absence,
a world he isn't *in.*

4. Beyond Necessity

You choke on grief, that's what people say.

I'm the one the others all reproach
for coldness, lack of exhibition.
Oh-I-know-you-have-as-many-feelings,
said my mother once.

How do you do it?

5. And Then

They'll take a blade and make an incision in his chest.

They'll take his lung or lungs out with their tools,
install the new.

Weeks of waiting and, almighty hope, recovery.

Then maybe he's restored, becomes
a man who's shed his Tube, who jogs
to get the ringing phone, who throws a football standing up,
spiral after spiral, out there in the grass with all the little kids.

Waiting, at First

The phone call now is in the air–
hovering above the Eastern seaboard,
ready to divide all time
into Doomed and Undoomed, ready
to jingle into their kitchen
and split the air like a shot,
like water breaking:
Grab the suitcase;
race to the hospital–

     spacious, state-of-the-art surgical theaters

     sophisticated cardiothoracic ICU

     postoperative floor care provided on Milstein 7

which sounds like a spaceship
or a rock band.

They will watch him for *obliterative
bronchiolitis,* afterward. And it goes on, this portioning
of hope, this freighting hope with variables, contingencies:
                    whatever this feeds, whatever it solicits

it also throttles, clots. I put the brochure down.

Brochure–can that be what it's called?

Those are just words: *locus mismatch.*

Sticky ones, like a dream
you have to will away, and not just will:
you need your body to participate.
I put the pages down; I walk away
from my desk, the window framing its cactus–
an Organ Pipe, the kind without thorns.

I should cook. I get the cucumber, the carrots,

I split off the cabbage's rubbery leaves,
I julienne.

Almost singing now,

No locus mismatch, *no locus mismatch, no locus mismatch–*

One Story of Conversion

I was trying to tell my neighbor about Saint Eustace,
he thought I was talking about
the guy just east of us—
who rotated the sprinklers on the front lawn
and then, strolling in a nearby park,
had an out-of-body experience.

Eustace was in the woods, I said;
he wore tights. Of course he had dogs
and a sheepskin canteen.
He saw Jesus, hanging
between the antlers of a deer. He had merely
meant to go walking,
maybe shoot himself some dinner.
The forest was prickly, thicker than he remembered.
The dogs couldn't be their usual breakneck selves.
He thought of whistling to them, of turning back.

He saw no landmarks,
could not locate that particularly wide pine
or the peak that rose up so sharply, like a horse's neck.
Just picture that—Eustace looking around.
And then, suddenly, straight ahead of him:
the motionless buck,
staring into his face with unstartled brown eyes,
supporting this miniature Christ
who was still dying.

Eustace fell to his knees, hugging himself
tightly into a ball.
The dogs nuzzled him frantically.
He jerked himself up, wanting to see again—
Eustace is famous for this, his story
was well received once he made his way home.

That's what I told him. But I think
he was bored–couldn't see it,
Eustace plunging downhill, elated, terrified
as the path cleared itself, brambles
and vines like snakes drawing back, and then, too,
the buck following, the blur of his hooves winging over the ground.

Went to Bed without a Blanket

I wake indoors, but to an utterly black
night swimming in the window,
pushing the lace panels toward the bed,
and this breeze: such a full
shocking touch, my body strains
to be subsumed.

My head has risen
from the pillow–my face I know
gone slack, the gods now vanished
and my body cooling,
leaning toward their exit.

Alembic

We ordered from a catalog a yellow rose,
an alchemist. They'll grow here in the desert
if you tinker with the soil. As if this grit
were soil.... We dig and scrape all morning,
working the smaller shovel like a pick.
The labor brings us in and out of unison:
such a struggle, thorny bare-root shrub.

Things a Depressed Person Cannot Do

Wait in line at the Division of Motor Vehicles.
Purchase mayonnaise.
Speak a foreign language.

Tolerate   an infant;
                a spouse's story-of-the-day;
                more than one noise at a time (voice + dishwasher, say,
                                    or TV + magazine page);
                any noise in a room with a tile floor;
                synthetic fabric, especially on the skin of the arms.

Nor: Tease

                 Protect

                 Console

                 Seduce

Candle under Glass

1. The Question

I drove home tonight
    (by myself, from a picnic,
    up to our house in the foothills)

full of joy
    (singing in the car,
    the mountains the muted purple
    of Sonoran dusk, the CD a gift
    from someone who knows
    I am happy)
mostly, generally, reliably.

What can it possibly mean
that I am happy
when the person I love
has no capacity for happiness?

2. The Kind of Argument

I want to talk about the guitars.
You want to talk about the children.
Fuck it.

Our impasse.

3. The Kind of Trouble

I would like to go to bed with someone
who is glad to be alive.

4. Safety Clasp

So far, I only imagine this with people who are married well,
not going anywhere. Who maybe, because they're honest,
notice a little heat, a little mutual noticing, but–

no threat. Both sides alive to each other,
sated, really, just by that.

But what I imagine: begins
with an admittedly fatherly embrace,

from which hungrily, I–

No. Frequently what I imagine proceeds directly from

hungrily, I–

5. The Candle under Glass Appears and Disappears

It is not true
that you would always rather be dead.

I know my list won't help you–
my list of your attachments, proof by travelogue,
or proof by belly laugh,
by any set of thrill citations: no one really remembers awe (for example)–
it's not retrievable;
in memory, it's always fogged, for all of us.

But I am telling you:
you would not *always rather be dead*.
Wrap that in whatever faith is left in you.
The world will enter you again.
You will unfold beneath the stars and see the sky.
(You'll be with me.)

Nocturnal

Their bedroom window's open one flight up—
I used to panic when boys walked me
to the porch, what might they hear?
Now, we come outside for Mike to smoke
and I wonder how deep asleep they are,
if they can smell it, if our quiet evening voices
offer just a murmur or a cause to strain
and try to hear.

We imagine our new house,
or rented rooms, how many rooms?
By the river or closer to the town
that only one of us so far has seen?
In June we'll take a trip to look together.
For now, indulgence, fantasy: a tub with feet,
claws curved against white tiles, a window wide
and low—long view.

We lapse into impossible desires—other states,
whole farms with horses, plots of vegetables.
We laugh too loud and hear a cough—polite,
requesting, and then my mother laughs herself.
Come on, I call, *come out!* The sash creaks further up,
and down around the roof my father's voice:
he hasn't been awake this late in years,
nor had a cigarette, has got to work tomorrow.
My mother joins him at the screen and says,
Look—half a moon.

We four all listen to each other
though there's nothing much to hear. I am imagining
the way they look, my mom's blue nightgown
loose and falling toward the sill, my father
in his pj's kneeling so his face can reach the air.
It's an easy blessing to inhabit, facing all

the darkened windows down the street,
each one of us a different calm, remembering
a different time that holds us here inside the presence
we are making, our partners close at hand and then the other pair
we cannot see.

City Hospital

What do you want most?

To see inside the hospital.
Ten years empty, housing projects on one side,
sturdy neighborhood on the other: windows smashed,
asphalt gnarled with weeds.
The high wailing dirty windows
open to the city night, the poison rain.

The city wants to use the space for something else,
to dynamite and haul away the ruined mass, the rooms and corridors,
places to wait, places to scrub or cut or watch over.
Places to fill out forms, places to eat and launder and inject.

Anyone in there now?

Birds go in.

And you–

People say it scares them, makes a noise,
sends its ominous presence snaking into passing cars.
They'll run the light in order not to linger.

And you expect to see?

I have two dreams. In one, every hall and room
is empty. Dropping ceilings, bits of things that blow in,
evidence of birds. Nothing else.
The tile is chipped, the floors weak
from water and the rot of time.

Two.

Archeology: equipment in shambles,
rubber tubes, steel pans and tongs and instruments,

monitors hanging from their wires off the walls.
Cafeteria trays, scraps of linens,
plastic chairs reconfigured by the various
unhappy trespassers–eight years ago,
six months ago, this morning.
The sounds inside the building–
muffled traffic, pigeons clucking, ruffle of wings
and flight. Something breaking, falling
now, even as we step. The grit under our shoes.
An ancient-building creak, a siren,
the not-quite-echo aftersound of my own movements, yours.
Debris and dust and someone's personal effects:
empty cans of corn and beans, chip bags, quarts of beer.
A sweatshirt slung across a counter top,
cardboard and newspaper underneath, the place he slept.

There must have been a morgue.

You see the fascination.

There must have been great furnaces,
elevators, blood storage, refrigeration.
There must have been a morgue.

A hospital given over to the dead, or death itself.
Except the birds. The place run through
with wind, a skeleton, a source
of silence, the kind of silence
made frightening by interruption, by any tiny sound.

What tiny sound?

The sound of us, the human sound.

Eucharistic

for R.H., A.H., A.R., C.S., & K.G.

The cup of luck is what we pass
on Friday nights–it looks like lousy wine
in paper party fixings, plus a certain someone's
plastic stemware–but it's luck
or lucky love.

Our eighteen kids–eighteen!–
sneak out into the desert,
the big ones smashing rocks
in search of crystals, the smaller ones
more closely tethered, on their bikes
and trikes. If you're like me

you don't know how this happened:
we were six people with six kids,
and now we're sisters in a family
that's a city: fortress, temple,
pleasure dome, arena . . . the children
manning every outpost: soldier/archeologist,
neurasthenic princess/teepee architect:
each one so many more than one,
so much herself. Or him-.

We'd never have been friends
without them, as we know, and marvel
privately. But here we are,
baked in the one loaf.

Night Dances

I thought I lived outside such music,
watching my beloved, yes, sure, gripped
or loosened, loosening and tightening his grip–

but there are darks into which
I find myself unloosed, pitched.
The chords thrumming in my chest a sick

careen from settled to unloosed.
It seems serene enough at first.
Fine to be wakeful and attentive, lost

at heart inside some song, aroused,
sentient in each swelling little vesicle–
then that knowledge goes all sour, soured

by anxiety and lust, anxiety not tamed by lust,
the self its own thick frame and limit,
and the soul at play against those walls, a ghost.

Dissolution

I am now sensible that I must withdraw from your acquaintance, and see neither you nor the rest of my friends any more, if I may but leave them quietly.
　　　　　　–Newton in a letter to Samuel Pepys, September 1693

I.

Newton's life moved toward
and then away from one point:
at first, experiment and investigation

(he wrote Halley, "I keep the subject constantly before me
and wait till the first dawnings open slowly, by little and little,
into a full and clear light");

later, public life: London, the presidency of the Royal Society,
warden and then Master of the Mint.

In between: the "Black Year," the vicious madness.

Writing to Pepys and to John Locke,
full of his fear of "embroilment":

Locke had endeavoured to embroil him with women,
and Pepys, he feared, with favor-seeking,

accusatory, vituperative–

Then it went away. He apologized,
told Locke he'd wished him dead
but didn't mean it.

The letters they exchanged
were loving letters,

Locke: *I am more ready to forgive you*
than you can be to desire it–

II.

His house was furnished all in red and black
(nine black leather chairs, two square glasses
in black frames) and gold–gilded mirror
in his bedroom, over the chimney.

Away–*away*–dark warren of the mind.

Five pairs of crimson mohair window vallance cornishes,
a crimson mohair bed complete with case curtains of crimson Harrateen,
the crimson mohair hangings of the room lined with canvas,
a crimson sattee cushion,
a crimson easy chair and case,
six crimson cushions filled with down,
a small India skreen, thirteen India prints–

III.

Resurgence of capacity:
he answered Pepys' fretting
with formulae, helping his friend
enumerate some odds, a probability for dice rolls.

Everything *fixed*. Betting on recovery
we calculate; we pause, assigning values.

What we wait for:

the willingness to be forgiven
to rise up full and clear in those we love.

Slope

We walk across the parking lot after the movie
confessing fears to each other and laughing
at their sameness.
The air is full of piped-in music,
even out here, where for a moment
we lean against the car
like teenagers, my jeans against your jeans,
and you say, looking overhead,
It's never silent anywhere anymore,
and then the noise wins: we're too old
or too self-conscious to be kissing
under the yellow lights, *to the tune of–*

Still: we are each other's
again, for the first time in so long.

Knowledge like oxygen, unremarkable
until it's threatened, returning like a kind of saturation,
though you can't feel either one
in your pores, your fingertips–

In the morning, I go out early and walk
between the rows of houses. I'm mailing a letter
and sending off the bills. It's not
a tree-lined street; it's mostly
scrubby low-slung thorns. So the morning light
is never filtered by a canopy of oaks or sycamores;
it's bright and hot and bearing down,
and rain has made the sage smell sweet,
and I can see for miles across the valley–
beyond the arc that Bell Road makes,
I can see the peaks and shoulders of the mountains
that bound the other side from mine.

Entreaty to the Air

The proof of beauty is in its making,
its recurrence: *we want it.*

Or in the heart's ability to lift
& plummet, simultaneously.
That much, beauty shares with nausea.

Any point can be one of intersection.

I want my father to move again without calculation,
I want my husband to laugh and sleep,
my tiny son's tiny heart not to murmur anymore.

I used to look for omens, was the target
of disappointment, as if I sought it....

Now I look into the air, asking,
Enter us. Become everything air
is always turning into—unfurling string of thought,
signature of a met gaze, athletic arch of the back....

Oh: we are petty, or we are goofing off. We argue,
or we touch each other briefly in passing, touch, say, a bicep,
through the poplin sleeve, cupping it in a palm, grip of the fingers
on the slightly flexing muscle.
You are the air,
be this kind of matter.

Notes

Gottfried Wilhelm Leibniz was born in 1646 in Leipzig, Germany. Isaac Newton was born Christmas Day in 1642 outside of Grantham, England. As young men they approximately simultaneously, independently invented the calculus. Over time they were drawn into a fierce priority dispute in which the stakes were not only credit for the mathematical discovery but national intellectual supremacy.

Leibniz spent his life a diplomat, attached to various dukes, negotiating all manner of tricky stalemates: alliances within the Germanic territories, the potential reunion of the Catholic and Protestant churches, other suitable (non-German) targets for French aggression, say, Morocco... He was convivial; he enjoyed robust meals; he moved in busy, gossipy social circles, and maintained enormous correspondence with friends and colleagues all over Europe and the world–defending "Asiatics" against charges of atheism, for example, and hoping to gain credence for his own ideogrammatic symbols by introducing them in China.

Leibniz was discarded by King George, and when he died, under virtual house arrest near the banks of the Leine River, there were no mourners save his secretary, George Eckhart, who saw to the funereal details: armorial bearing and dates of birth and death inscribed at one end of the coffin, a phoenix consumed in fire at the other.

Notes about particular poems

"Notebook," "Violent Motion," "Odours and Vapours," "Gravity and Levity," "Memory":
As a student Newton kept a notebook, *Questiones Quædam Philosophicæ, Some Philosophical Questions,* a collection of problems, theories, potential experiments, and sometimes aesthetic or psychological ruminations. These poems take their titles from Newton's headings in this notebook. The opening of "Memory" quotes Newton directly.

"Annus Mirabilis"
Leibniz's "Insight must be joined to fervour" appears in the *Theodicy*;
Newton's "Fantasy is helped . . ." appears in his *Questiones* notebook.

"Function of X"
Some quotations attributed to X are actually from John Nash, as quoted by
Sylvia Nasar in *A Beautiful Mind* (Simon and Schuster, 1998) and from
Nash's Nobel acceptance speech.

"Dissolution"
The items listed in section two are culled from a postmortem inventory
compiled by Hannah Thompson, April 24,1727.

Acknowledgments

Grateful acknowledgment is made to the editors of the following journals in which some of these poems first appeared, sometimes in different forms:

"Annus Mirabilis"
"Newton's Death Mask"
"Proofs"
"Toward the Opticks"
"Violent Motion"   *Barrow Street*

"City Hospital"   *The Bellevue Literary Review*

"Candle under Glass"   *Boulevard*

"f(N) = 6(s + 7)"
"Function of X"
"In Hannover: Clairvoyance"   *Drunken Boat*

"The Old Neighborhood"
"Went to Bed without a Blanket"   *The Four Way Reader #2*

"Water and Salt"   *Haydens Ferry Review*

"Ascent"   *Marlboro Review*

"Memory"   *Ploughshares*

"Slope"   *Rivendell*

"Creation of the World"   *Salmagundi*

"1652"   *Slate*

"Nocturnal"   *Southwest Review*

"Trinket"   *Spoon River Poetry Review*

"Grown Son"
"One Story of Conversion"   *Threepenny Review*

"Nocturnal" was reprinted in *The Best American Poetry*, edited by David Lehman and Richard Howard (Scribner, 1995).

∫

Love and gratitude to Louise Glück, Robert Hahn, and Chris Nealon for close readings of this book in progress; and to Ellen Bryant Voigt for her bracing and generous attention. Thanks also to Peter Covino, Rob Drummond, Melissa Hotchkiss, and everyone at Barrow Street Press. Thank you Elizabeth Andersen, Heide Ziegler, Susan Lang, and Martha Rhodes. Ted, Celia, & Oscar: mirabilis indeed.
To Mike McNally, true love: [x,o].

Sally Ball's poems have appeared in *Ploughshares, Slate, Threepenny Review,* and *The Best American Poetry* anthology, and her prose in *Pleiades* and the *Review of Contemporary American Fiction.* She is the senior editor of Four Way Books.